FOREST COMMUNITIES
Living in Harmony with Fire

THE **WHIZPOPS**

Illustrated by Glory Lawson

2017

Mountain Press Publishing Company

Missoula, Montana

Text © 2017 by the Whizpops
Illustrations © 2017 by Glory Lawson

First Printing, April 2017
All rights reserved

Library of Congress Cataloging-in-Publication Data

Names: Cashman, Kevin, 1981- , author. | Lawson, Glory, 1974- , illustrator.
 | Whizpops.
Title: Forest communities : living in harmony with fire / The Whizpops ;
 illustrated by Glory Lawson.
Description: Missoula, Montana : Mountain Press Publishing Company, 2017. |
 Based on a song by the band The Whizpops. | Audience: Ages 6 and up.
Identifiers: LCCN 2016056344 | ISBN 9780878426744 (cloth : alk. paper)
Subjects: LCSH: Pine—Effect of fires on—West (U.S.)—Juvenile literature. |
 Fire ecology—West (U.S.)—Juvenile literature.
Classification: LCC SD397.P55 C28 2017 | DDC 634.9/751—dc23
LC record available at https://lccn.loc.gov/2016056344

PRINTED IN HONG KONG

MP Mountain Press
PUBLISHING COMPANY
P.O. Box 2399 • Missoula, MT 59806 • 406-728-1900
800-234-5308 • info@mtnpress.com
www.mountain-press.com

When you walk into the woods,
stop and look around.

There's an easy way to tell
which forest you've found!

There's a whole world of forests to smell and to see!

Today, we're only going to talk about three.

Three pine trees—the ponderosa, lodgepole, and whitebark pines—form three distinctive forests in the West. Each of these trees and their forest communities have developed their own unique ways to get along with forest fires. Although some fires can be dangerous and destructive, pines are well adapted to live with fire. Fire helps these forests thrive.

PONDEROSA

LODGEPOLE

WHITEBARK

Ponderosa pines stand lonely but proud.
Lodgepole pines grow up in big crowds.
Whitebark pine twists and it bends,
high up in the mountains with a whole lot of friends!

The ponderosa pine likes dry, warm sites in
valleys and foothills. The lodgepole pine seeks
out moister sites higher in the mountains than the
ponderosa pine. The whitebark pine survives near
timberline on steep mountain ridges. Each tree
has a favorite place to live, just like people.

Thick bark, big trunk,
branches reaching high . . .

I must be standing with
the ponderosa pine!

Ponderosa pines can grow more than 150 feet tall and live for hundreds of years. Some old trees have huge trunks that are as big around as a circle formed by you and five or six of your friends holding hands! The thick bark, which protects the tree from fire, looks like pieces of a jigsaw puzzle. Native Americans peeled the bark in spring to eat the sugary inner layer. Try scratching the bark of an old ponderosa pine and sniffing its vanilla or butterscotch scent.

Pileated woodpecker, white-tailed deer . . . Arrowleaf balsamroot are "lichen" it here!

Healthy ponderosa pine forests have widely spaced trees with lots of grassy areas in between. The forest floor is sunny, warm, and inviting; it's a good place for animals, wildflowers, and humans to live. Lichen is a tiny plant growing together with a fungus. Look for lichen growing in spots upon the bark of ponderosas.

Elk munching bunchgrass,
lots of room for birds to fly . . .

This forest is healthy, and I
think I know the reason why!

Slow-moving, creepy-crawly fires burn
the grass and pine needles on the ground in
ponderosa pine forests. These low-intensity fires don't
harm the big, thick-barked trees. Fires may scorch the outside of
the bark, but before it can burn too deeply, thin, platy pieces of the
smoldering bark fall off and land on the burned ground below. The removal of
the burning bark from the tree trunk prevents the entire tree from catching on fire. These
surface fires kill young Douglas-fir trees, which thrive in shade and often invade the open
ponderosa forests. Fires every five to ten years keep the forest clear of the pesky fir.

Every living thing
growing in the woods
agrees that forests need
fire to live in harmony!

There will always be another
seed to grow underneath.
It's the never-ending cycle
of forest communities!

After the fire is out and the ground has cooled, bunchgrasses, low plants, and shrubs send up new green shoots from their deep roots. Elk and deer love these tender shoots. Unlike the grasses and deep-rooted perennial flowers like arrowleaf balsamroot, Douglas-fir saplings do not sprout after fire. The ponderosa pine community is a welcoming place soon after a fire!

Branches weaving together,
blocking out the sky . . .
I must be standing with the lodgepole pine!

Tall, skinny trunks, serotinous cones . . .
just waiting there to open 'til the
fire comes home!

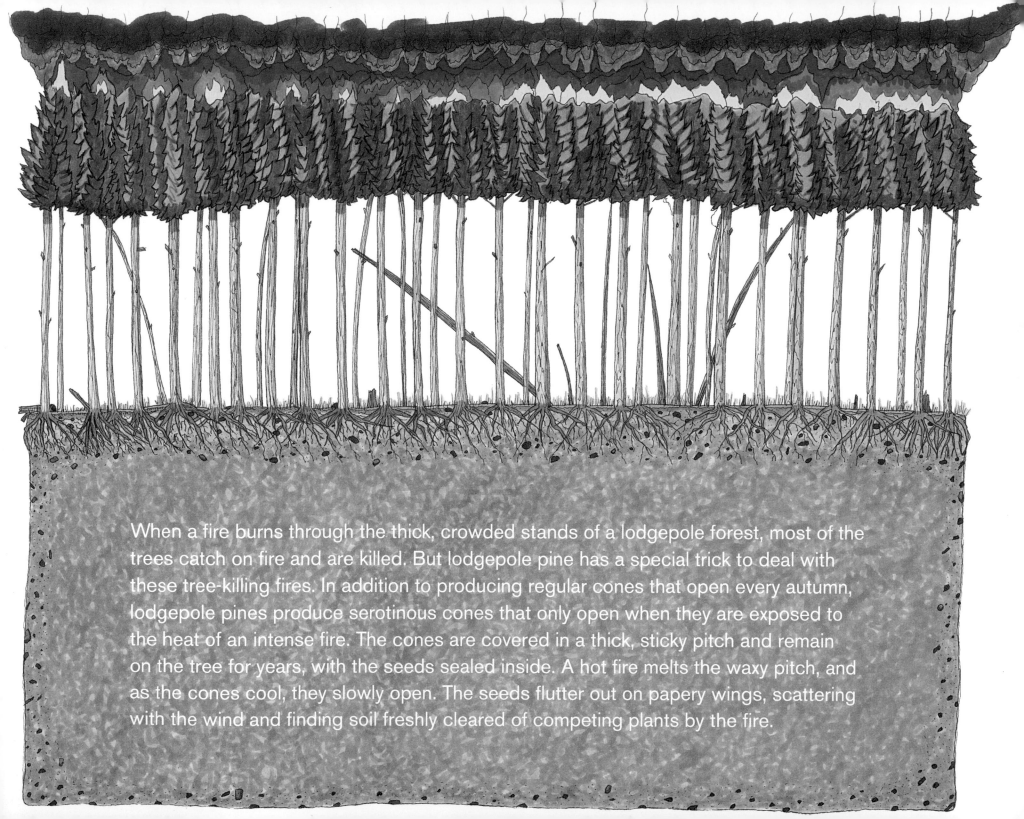

When a fire burns through the thick, crowded stands of a lodgepole forest, most of the trees catch on fire and are killed. But lodgepole pine has a special trick to deal with these tree-killing fires. In addition to producing regular cones that open every autumn, lodgepole pines produce serotinous cones that only open when they are exposed to the heat of an intense fire. The cones are covered in a thick, sticky pitch and remain on the tree for years, with the seeds sealed inside. A hot fire melts the waxy pitch, and as the cones cool, they slowly open. The seeds flutter out on papery wings, scattering with the wind and finding soil freshly cleared of competing plants by the fire.

Beneath this canopy is a great
place for critters to hide.
This forest is healthy, and I
think I know the reason why!

Lodgepole pines can't grow in the shade of other plants. After a severe fire kills all the competing trees and shrubs, lodgepole seedlings can thrive. In the spring following a fire, the seeds sprout into tiny green trees. They love the sun, so they grow straight up—and fast—before other trees can shade them out. Lodgepole pine forests have large numbers of trees that are the same age because they all started growing together in the same year!

Every living thing growing in the woods agrees
that forests need fire to live in harmony!

There will always be another seed
to grow underneath.

It's the never-ending cycle
of forest communities!

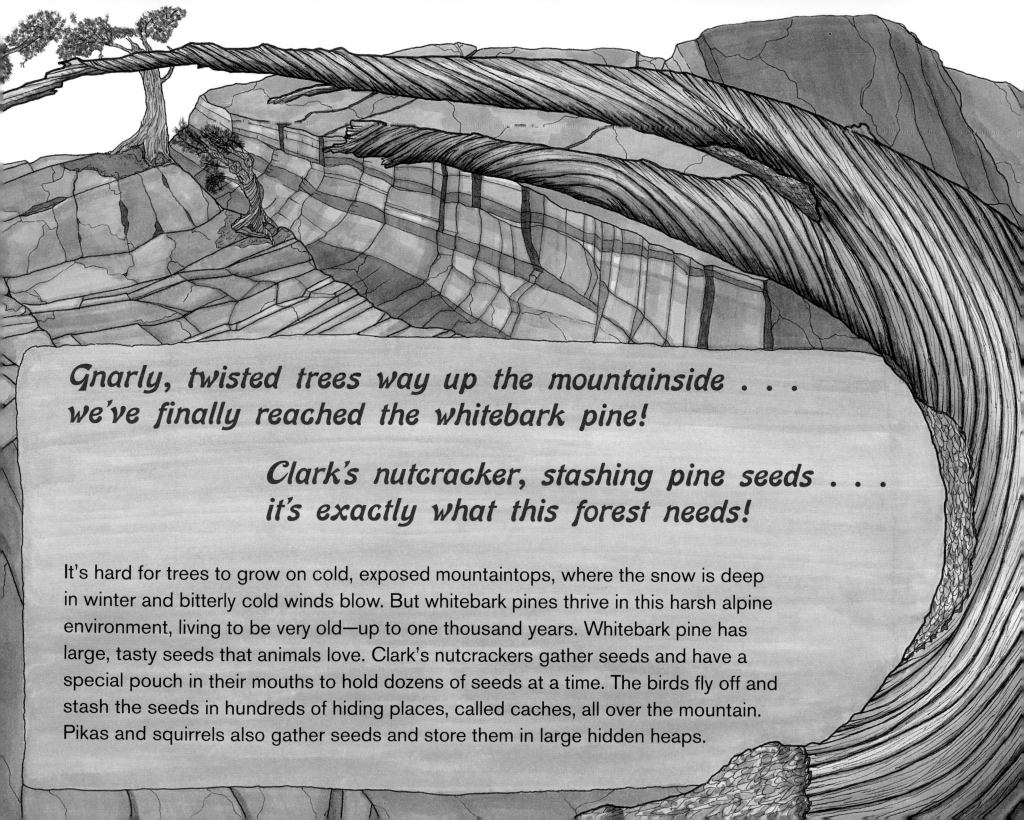

Gnarly, twisted trees way up the mountainside . . .
we've finally reached the whitebark pine!

Clark's nutcracker, stashing pine seeds . . .
it's exactly what this forest needs!

It's hard for trees to grow on cold, exposed mountaintops, where the snow is deep in winter and bitterly cold winds blow. But whitebark pines thrive in this harsh alpine environment, living to be very old—up to one thousand years. Whitebark pine has large, tasty seeds that animals love. Clark's nutcrackers gather seeds and have a special pouch in their mouths to hold dozens of seeds at a time. The birds fly off and stash the seeds in hundreds of hiding places, called caches, all over the mountain. Pikas and squirrels also gather seeds and store them in large hidden heaps.

Eating these seeds will help the grizzly bear survive.

This forest is healthy, and I think
I know the reason why!

Whitebark pine has fairly thick bark and survives most fires. It doesn't survive competition from other trees, though, so fire helps keep whitebark pine forests open and healthy. Fire also clears away excess plant material so seedlings have a better chance of surviving. Clark's nutcrackers like to bury seeds in soil exposed by fire, which are great places for seedlings to grow. Animals usually cache more seeds than they can possibly eat, leaving some to become future trees. Grizzly bears find some of the seed caches and feast on them before winter!

Fires in the high country burn like roller coasters, creeping slowly around the ground, finding brush, climbing up, and even jumping into the trees! Then they drop down and move slowly around until they run out of fuel in a rocky patch, or rain and snow come and quench the heat. After alpine fires, whitebark pine are often the first trees to regenerate.

Every living thing growing in the woods agrees that forests need fire to live in harmony!

There will always be another seed to grow underneath.

It's the never-ending cycle of forest communities!

Living with Wildfires

In the old days, fires burned regularly through many western forests. Frequent fires kept the forests clear of dead wood and small trees, so the fires were mostly slow-burning, smoldering affairs. People have been preventing fires for so long now that when a forest does catch on fire, it literally goes up in flames. During the heat of the summer, forest fires start easily from lightning, sparks from engines, and untended campfires. There's so much fuel in today's forests that even large ponderosa pines are killed by the heat and intensity of the fires. The current trend of hotter, drier summers also plays an important role in today's severe wildfires.

A fire needs three things to burn: fuel, heat, and oxygen. Scientists call this the fire triangle, and if you take away one side of this triangle, the fire will stop burning. It's pretty hard to take away the summer's heat and the oxygen in the air, but fuel can be reduced. During cool weather in fall, winter, and spring, foresters use fire to reduce the fuel in forests. These fires are called prescribed fires—they make the forest healthier, just like a drug prescribed by your doctor can make you healthier. Foresters carefully tend prescribed fires so they don't get out of control. Foresters also need help from loggers to thin forests that have grown too thick in the absence of fire.

Fire is a natural part of the ecosystem in the West. Like the adaptable pine trees, we can find ways to plan for and live with fires within our communities. We can thin our backyard forests, rake up pine needles and cones, and make our houses out of fireproof material. As long as we do our part to keep the forests healthy, these forest communities will continue to thrive for many years to come!

OXYGEN

HEAT

FUEL

Glossary

alpine. The upper part of mountains where few trees grow.

arrowleaf balsamroot. A bright-yellow flower in the sunflower family.

bunchgrass. A type of grass that grows in tufts.

cache. A hiding place where squirrels and other animals store seeds and other food.

canopy. The highest layer of branches and leaves on a tree or in a forest.

Clark's nutcracker. A gray, white, and black bird that lives in the mountains of western North America.

cycle. Events that occur over and over in the same or similar pattern.

fire triangle. A fire needs three things in order to burn: fuel, heat, and oxygen.

gnarly. Rough, worn, or weathered.

harmony. When different things work well together.

lichen. A tiny plant growing together with a fungus. Neither can live alone, but together they grow well, even on rocks and tree bark.

perennial. A plant that lives for many years.

pika. A small mammal that lives on rocky slopes on mountains.

pileated woodpecker. A very large woodpecker that lives in North America.

pitch. A sticky substance that is liquid when warm and hard when cold.

regenerate. To grow again, usually from seed.

serotinous cones. Pine cones that remain closed on the tree and open gradually or during the right conditions.

terrain. The natural features of an area of land.

understory. The layer of vegetation lying beneath the main canopy of a forest.

Resources

We composed our song "Forest Communities" as part of the score for the CoMotion Dance Project's "Fire Speaks the Land: An Active Audiences Performance." This live dance performance tours to schools and communities around the Rocky Mountain West and has been seen by ten thousand children, teachers, and parents. Here's a link to see the part of the show with our song: https://youtube.com/watch?v=scjC2Aab4a8.

For more information about the CoMotion Dance Project, visit comotiondanceproject.com.

If you want to learn more about fire science and ecology, visit the Missoula Fire Sciences Laboratory online and learn about their FireWorks educational program. There you'll find mountains of fun stuff to read and do: www.firelab.org/project/fireworks-educational-program.

Firewise.org, another online resource, provides practical tips, access to experts, teaching tools, and a kids' corner.

"What is a Flame?", an award-winning seven-minute video by Benjamin Ames, uses cartoons to illustate the nature of fire. Available at http://vimeo.com/40271657

About the Authors

The Whizpops are an award-winning educational band for families. Founded by two elementary school teachers, they have released several albums inspired by the natural world. Bridging songwriting with picture books helps reach young learners in multiple ways. The Whizpops can be found engaging kids of all ages from libraries to large venues in the Pacific Northwest. They are proud to call Missoula, Montana, their home and enjoy the energy and positive feedback from kids and parents alike. Listen to "Forest Communities" and other educational Whizpops music at www.thewhizpops.com.

About the Illustrator

Glory Lawson is a bachelor of fine arts candidate at the University of Montana and regularly exhibits her abstract paintings in her hometown of Missoula. She is the illustrator of *Talkin' Bout Dinosaurs*, also by the Whizpops. When she's not making art, she's working at a local kitchen shop, making jewelry, or singing and dreaming up new projects with her six-year-old daughter.